Dedication

**To the extraordinary folks at NASA with thanks and admiration
Special acknowledgement to my son, Peter, in Mission Control
at Johnson Space Center Houston, TX and to Mr. Kelly Humphries,
News Chief, NASA JSC**

Photo credits – NASA, Astronaut Cmdr. Scott Kelly and Jason Major, LightsInTheDark.com
Text copyright 2013, by Ann Morgan, M.Ed.
First Edition. The International Space Station by Ann Morgan

Summary: Vivid photographs and accessible text describe the International Space Station.
High interest, grades 2-3 reading level. ISBN 978-0-9773253-8-2 Starting Gate Press

Table of Contents

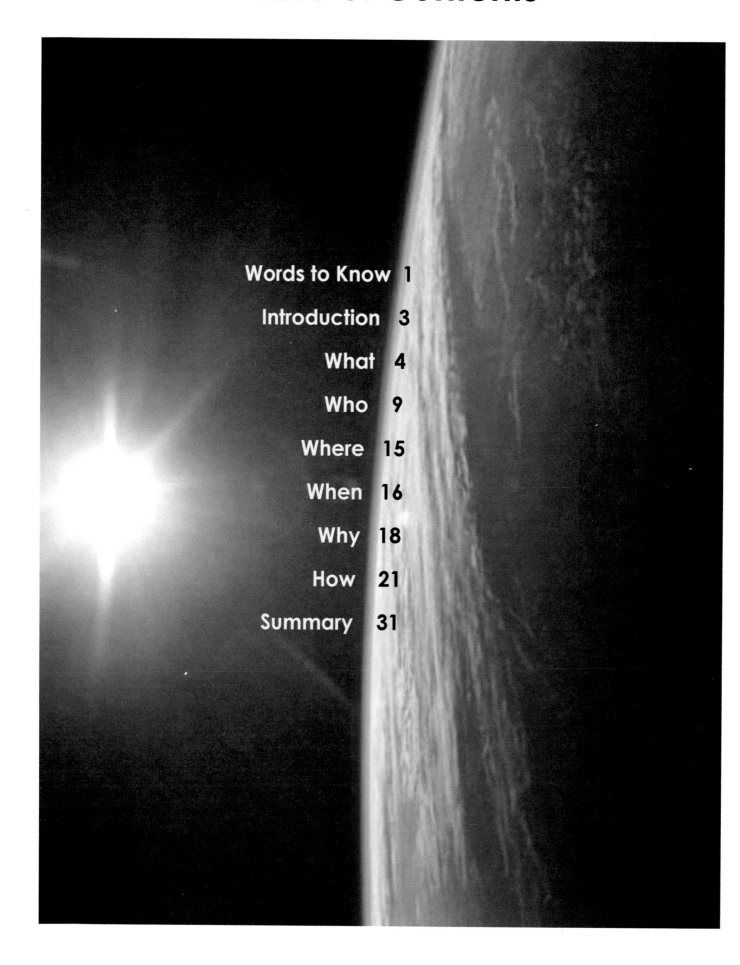

Words to Know

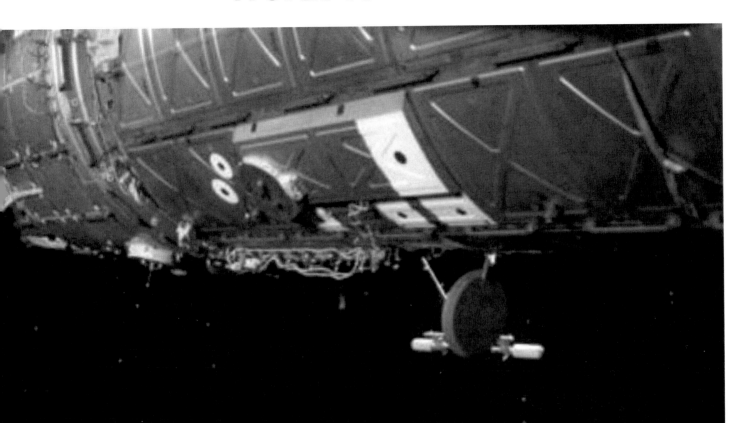

spacecraft	berthing port	gravity
orbit	airlock	crew compartment
human	solar panel	equipment
laboratory	solar array	spacesuit
experiment	international	jetpack
module	astronaut	safety cable
node	cosmonaut	Space Shuttle
supplies	crew	Soyuz
payload	space walker	rocket
docking port	mission control	

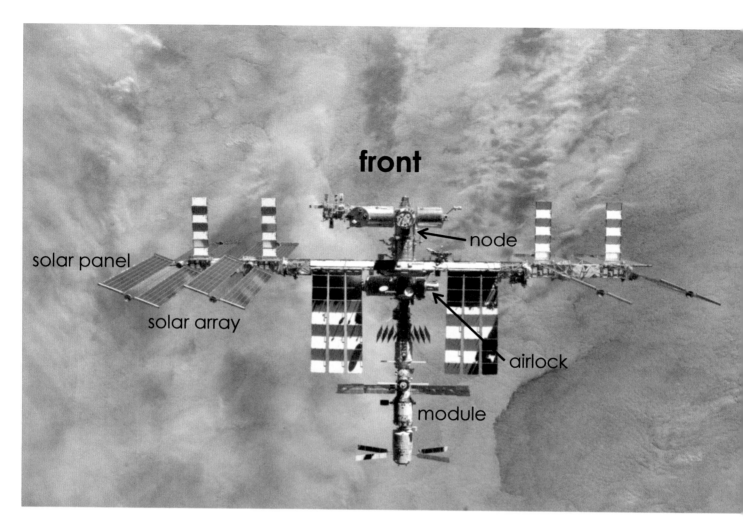

front

solar panel

solar array

node

airlock

module

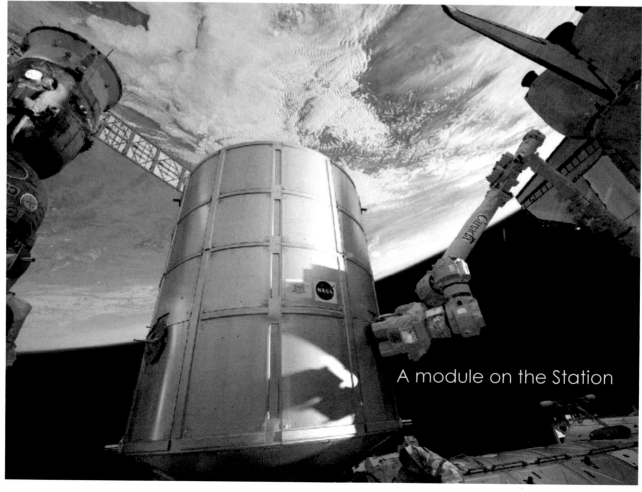

A module on the Station

Introduction

    The International Space Station is a **spacecraft** that goes around and around Earth. It orbits Earth at 17,500 miles an hour, or five miles every second. It is the largest man-made thing ever to **orbit** Earth. It is a place where people can work and live in space. It is a **human** spacecraft. The International Space Station is the only human spacecraft that can stay in space for many years. It has special rooms where people can work and rest.

What

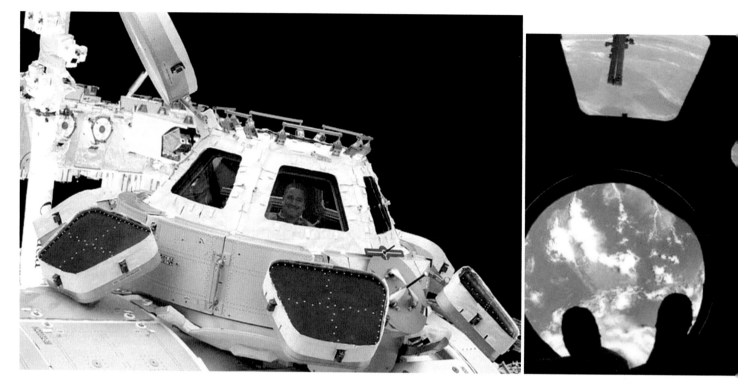

The Cupola is a module. It has windows all around and one on top.

The International Space Station is a big science **laboratory**. It is a place for people to try new ideas and learn new things. It is a place for **experiments**. It has 15 parts that are like rooms in a house. Some rooms are **modules**. Each module is a place for work or rest.

The Station has some places between modules. They are **nodes**. Nodes can connect other nodes and modules. Nodes are also places to work or rest. Station countries share modules and nodes.

Small spacecraft carry supplies to the International Space Station.

The Space Station needs things from Earth. It needs **supplies**. Other spacecraft carry the supplies up. They carry **payload**. They do not carry people. They park at **docking ports** or **berthing ports** on the Space Station. Each spacecraft stays at its port until it is time to leave.

The Space Station has special doors to the outside. The doors are **airlocks**. Airlocks keep good air in the spacecraft so the people inside can breathe.

Solar panels get energy from the sun for the International Space Station.

The International Space Station uses electricity. It gets electricity from the sun. The sun shines onto big flat pieces that stick out on the sides of the Station. Each piece is a **solar panel**. A group of solar panels is a **solar array**. Solar panels turn sun energy into electric energy.

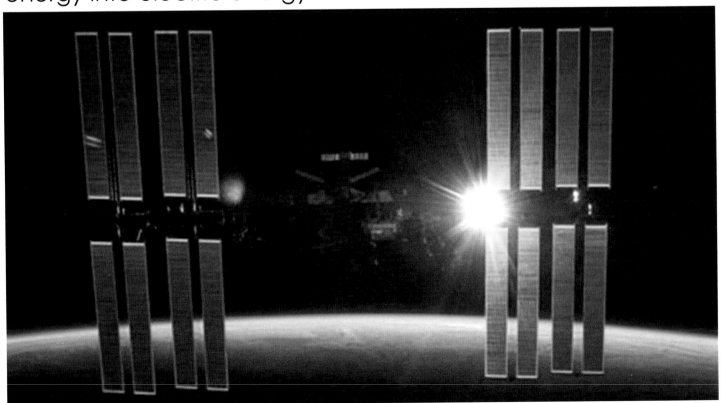

Canadarm2 is a giant robot arm on the International Space Station.

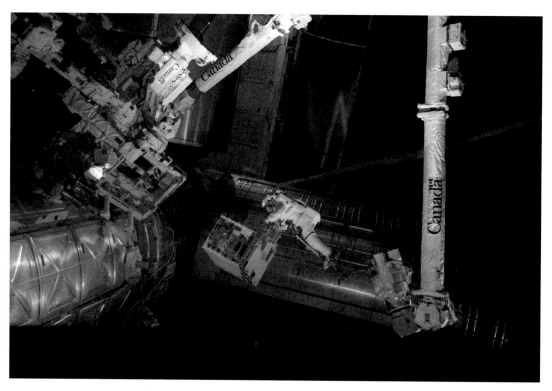

The International Space Station has a very long, very strong arm outside. It is a robot arm. People on Earth and people on the Station use computers to control the robot arm. It can bend. It can lift and hold big, heavy things to help spacecraft and people at the Station.

Who

These astronauts are getting ready to go into space.

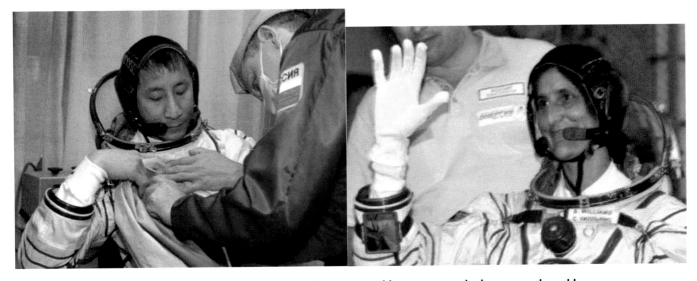

Fifteen countries from all over the world made the **International** Space Station. People who go to the Space Station are **astronauts** or **cosmonauts**. Cosmonauts work for Russia. Astronauts work for the other Space Station countries.

Some crew leave the Space Station when other crew arrive.

Six astronauts or cosmonauts can live on the International Space Station at the same time. They must practice on Earth for a long time before they can go to the Station. They train in the USA, Russia, Japan and parts of Europe. People on the Space Station at the same time are **crew**.

Member Countries and Control Centers

Countries That Have Sent Visitors to the Station*

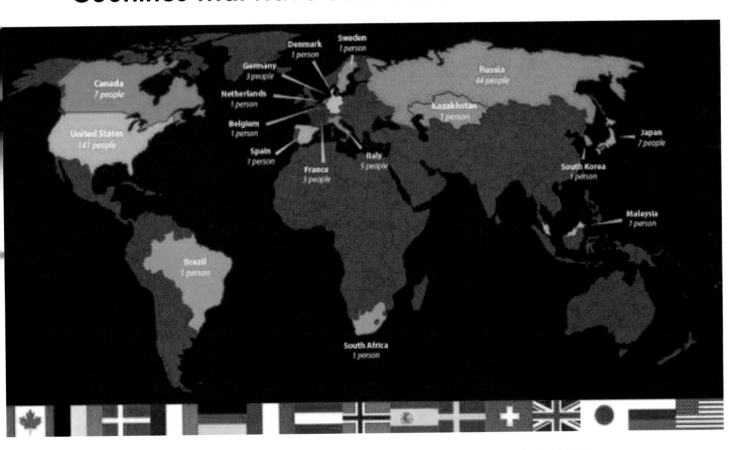

*An astronaut from Great Britain was added to this list in 2015

Countries of the International Space Station

The United States of America
NASA
National Aeronautical and Space
Administration

Russia
ROSCOSMOS
Russian Federal Space Agency

Belgium
ESA
European Space Agency

Norway
NSC/ESA
Norwegian Space Agency

Canada
CSA
Canadian Space Agency

The Netherlands
NSO / ESA
The Netherlands Space Office

Denmark
DNSC / ESA
Danish National Space Center

Spain
ESA
European space Agency

France
ESA
European Space Agency

Sweden
SNSB/ESA
Swedish National Space Board

Germany
ESA
European space Agency

Switzerland
SSO / ESA
Swiss Space Office

Italy
ISA / ESA
Italian Space Agency

The United Kingdom
UKSA/ESA
United Kingdom Space Agency

Japan
JAXA
Japanese Aerospace Exploration
Agency

Two NASA **spacewalkers**

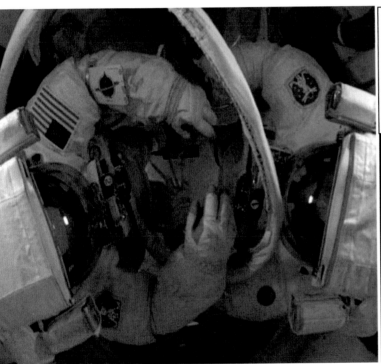

Every person on the Station has work to do. Sometimes people from the same country work together. Sometimes people from different countries work together.

People in Mission Control work together to keep the International Space Station safe.

People on Earth help the people on the International Space Station. They fly and control it from **Mission Control** on the ground. The people on Earth are Flight Controllers. They use computers and cameras to talk to the Station crew and help them do their jobs. They can see and hear almost everything on the spacecraft. They work at Mission Control Centers around the world.

Where

The International Space Station is in outer space where there is no air to breathe. It orbits about 250 miles above Earth. It goes all the way around the earth every 90 minutes. It is there every day and night, and it never stops. In the sky, only the sun and moon look brighter than the International Space Station.

Sometimes, on a dark, clear night, you can see the International Space Station. It looks like a small white dot sliding across the sky.

When

1998 – 2000

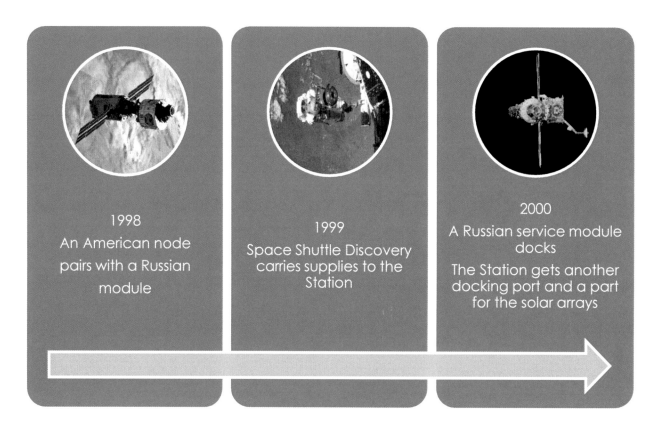

1998
An American node pairs with a Russian module

1999
Space Shuttle Discovery carries supplies to the Station

2000
A Russian service module docks

The Station gets another docking port and a part for the solar arrays

2001 – 2005

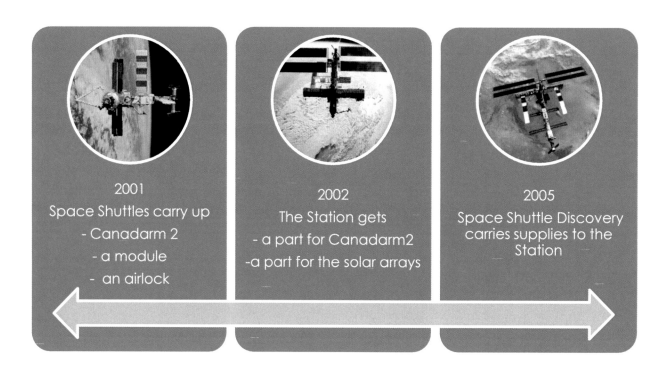

2001
Space Shuttles carry up
- Canadarm 2
- a module
- an airlock

2002
The Station gets
- a part for Canadarm2
- a part for the solar arrays

2005
Space Shuttle Discovery carries supplies to the Station

2006 – 2008

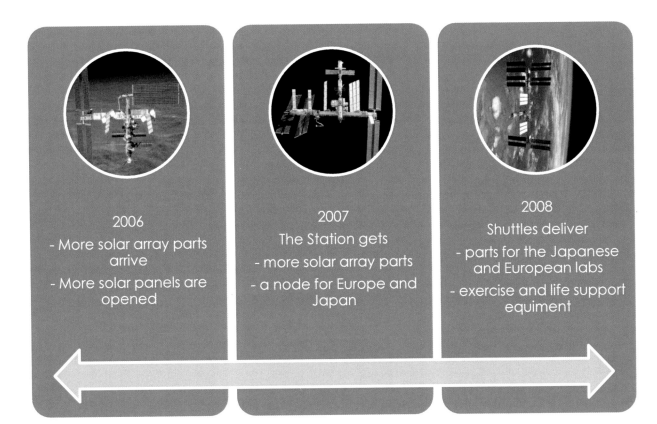

2006
- More solar array parts arrive
- More solar panels are opened

2007
The Station gets
- more solar array parts
- a node for Europe and Japan

2008
Shuttles deliver
- parts for the Japanese and European labs
- exercise and life support equiment

2009 – 2011

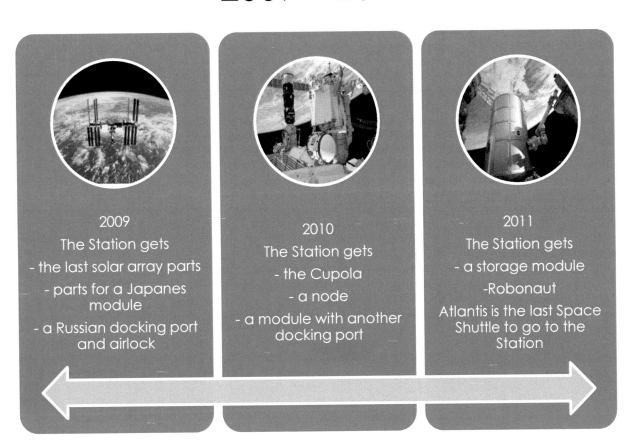

2009
The Station gets
- the last solar array parts
- parts for a Japanes module
- a Russian docking port and airlock

2010
The Station gets
- the Cupola
- a node
- a module with another docking port

2011
The Station gets
- a storage module
- Robonaut
Atlantis is the last Space Shuttle to go to the Station

Why

 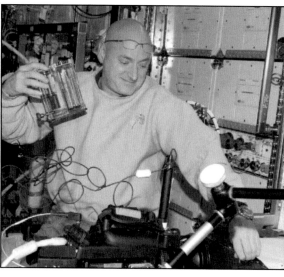 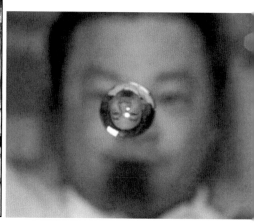

Work on the International Space Station is important for the world. It helps people learn ways to make life on Earth better. People on the Station can do jobs they cannot do on Earth. They test ways to live and work in outer space. The tests will help show people how to travel very very far into outer space and how to stay there for a long time.

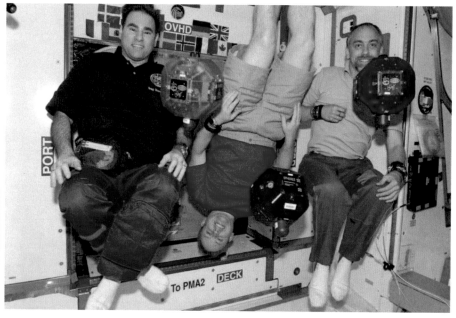

Up and down are different on the International Space Station. The deck faces Earth. It feels like there is no **gravity** on the International Space Station. Things do not fall.

A huge hurricane spins over the Atlantic Ocean and parts of Florida.

The Space Station has many cameras and computers. It can make pictures of almost any place on Earth. The pictures can show very big sections of land and water. They can show what happens from floods, fires, volcanoes, earthquakes and storms.

The International Space Station helps scientists study outer space.

A JAXA astronaut doing an oxygen experiment

Every job and experiment on the Space Station has a reason. Even making and using the Space Station is an experiment. Every job is to help understand something. People on the Space Station can:

- study the human body
- discover new things about outer space
- test new technology

- make stronger plants for food
- study Earth climate and weather
- teach about science, technology, math and engineering

How

Eat – There is no big refrigerator or stove on the Station, but there is a warming oven. Some food, like mashed potatoes or macaroni and cheese, is in special bags to put in the oven. Some food, like fruit or cookies, does not need special bags. The crew members eat with regular forks or spoons and use straws to drink. They must hold on to what they eat or it will float away.

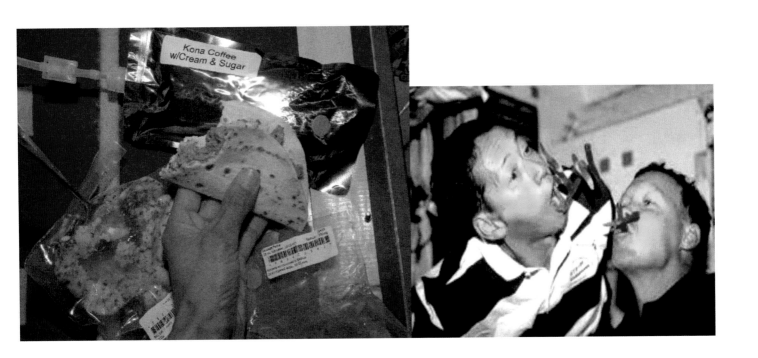

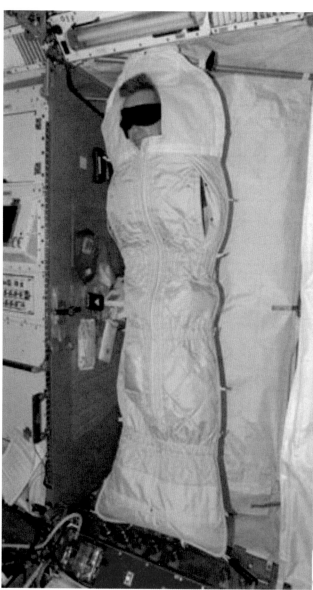

Sleep – People on the Station need sleep just like people on Earth. Each person has a sleeping bag tied to the wall in a small room. The small room is a **crew compartment**. Each crew compartment is big enough for just one person. Most crew members cover their eyes when they sleep because the sun comes up and shines in the windows every 90 minutes.

Exercise - People's bones and muscles change when they are in space. It is very important for crew to stay strong and healthy so they can do all of their jobs. They must exercise for at least two hours every day. They use straps to hold them onto the exercise **equipment**. They wear shoes inside only when they exercise.

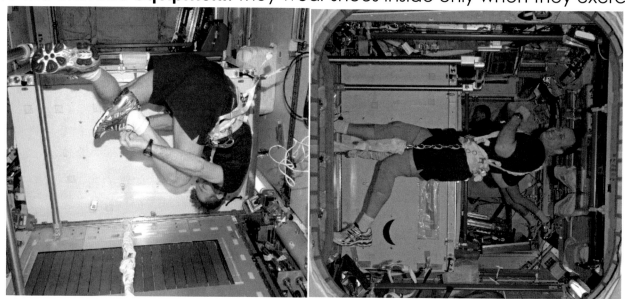

Use the bathroom and stay clean – Crew cannot use water on the Space Station like they do on Earth. They cannot shower or wash clothes. Each one must use a wet sponge or washcloth to get clean. They use soap and shampoo that they do not have to rinse off. They brush their teeth like on Earth, but they must swallow or spit into a washcloth.

The Station toilet is a little like a toilet on Earth. The toilet cannot use water. It uses air like a vacuum cleaner. The Space Station has two bathrooms. There is no way to get clothes clean on the station. Crew throw away their dirty clothes. They get clean ones from payload spaceships.

Equipment is tied down inside the Space Station. Crew is not.

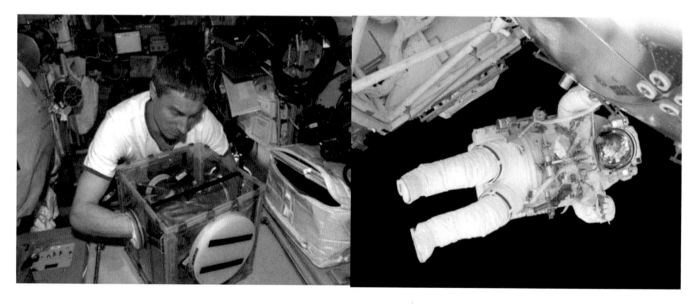

Work – Crew must learn new ways to work in tiny spaces inside and enormous space outside. They must hold on to bars with their hands and feet. They must know how to use special tools and equipment. Inside, they wear soft, loose clothes and no shoes. Outside, they wear big **spacesuits** that cover them all over. There is no air outside. Spacewalkers need oxygen tanks so they can breathe. Their helmets have a special covering so the sun cannot burn their eyes. Every spacesuit has a small **jetpack**. Spacewalkers use them to push back to the Station if they slip off.

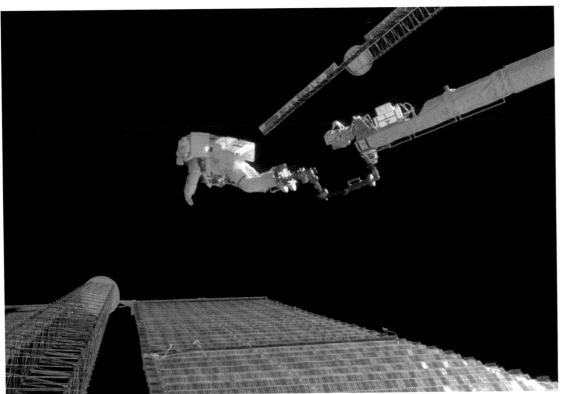

Crew who go outside the Space Station are tied to it with **safety cables.**

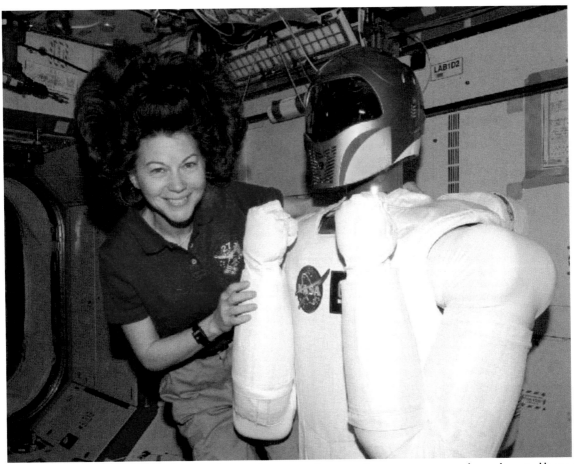

Robonaut is a robot made to help astronauts and cosmonauts when they are very busy. Robonaut can do jobs that are boring or that would make crew too tired. It can use the same tools and fit into the same spaces as a person.

Working at the International Space Station

Inside	Outside
soft, loose clothes	big, thick spacesuit
usually no special safety equipment	safety cables, oxygen, jetpacks, sun guard
can work alone	must have a partner
can take breaks	cannot take breaks
small equipment and machines	big equipment and machines

Relax – Each astronaut and cosmonaut may take a few small things to the Space Station. They do not have much room to put them away. They can take books, toys, musical instruments and other things that they like to use at home. Many space travelers take pictures and write notes about what they see and do. Space travelers like to celebrate holidays, birthdays, when crew arrive or leave, and to mark the number of days they have been on the Station. They use computers to visit and talk to their families and friends on Earth.

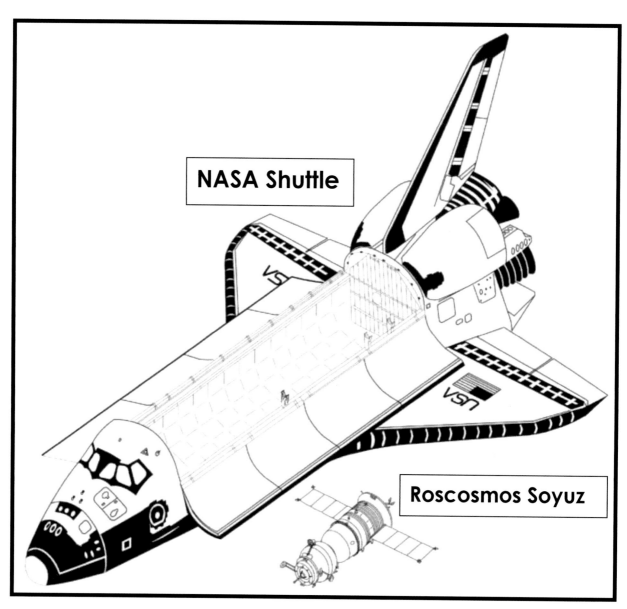

NASA Shuttle

Roscosmos Soyuz

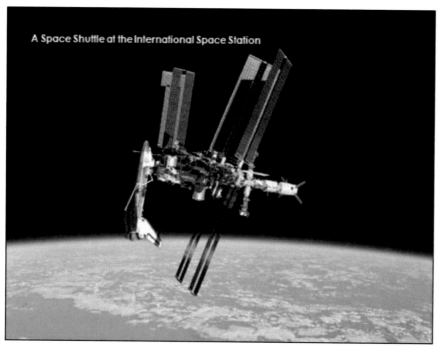

A Space Shuttle at the International Space Station

Travel – Space Station countries use crewed spaceships to get to the International Space Station. Giant **rockets** push them into outer space.

It can take from six hours to four days to get to the Space Station. The ships carry supplies and crew for the Space Station. When they finish their space jobs, crew members go back to Earth.

Soyuz launch

Shuttle launch

Roscosmos has the **Soyuz** for cosmonauts and astronauts. For now, all space travelers go up and return in the Soyuz. The Space Station always has at least one Soyuz ready to go, in case the crew has to leave fast.

NASA had the **Space Shuttle** until 2011. It went on over 100 missions. Different countries sent astronauts up on the Shuttle. Almost all of the huge parts on the International Space Station went up on Shuttles. Now NASA is building a new way to travel into outer space.

The Space Shuttle was huge so it could carry big things to and from the Space Station. It could hold seven people. Crew could look out windows in the front. It would leave the International Space Station, then circle Earth for a day or two. It landed like an airplane. A parachute behind it helped it stop. Shuttles were used many times.

The Soyuz is small . Only three people can fit inside. The Soyuz falls very fast from the Station through the sky. It takes less than four hours to reach Earth. It lands in the desert. A parachute makes it slow down. Each Soyuz is used only once.

Summary

The International Space Station is a science laboratory about 250 miles above the Earth. It is the 3rd brightest object in the night sky. It is the work of 15 countries that want to make life better and to explore past our Earth. People who work with the International Space Station are smart and brave. They do serious jobs. The International Space Station is one of the world's most important places to learn about what is all around us, on Earth and in outer space.

Made in the USA
Middletown, DE
15 October 2022

12857460R00020